TRAVELLING BEHIND GLASS

Anne Stevenson

TRAVELLING BEHIND GLASS

Selected Poems
1963-1973

London
OXFORD UNIVERSITY PRESS
New York Toronto
1974

Oxford University Press, Ely House, London W. 1

GLASGOW NEW YORK TORONTO MELBOURNE WELLINGTON
CAPE TOWN IBADAN NAIROBI DAR ES SALAAM LUSAKA ADDIS ABABA
DELHI BOMBAY CALCUTTA MADRAS KARACHI LAHORE DACCA
KUALA LUMPUR SINGAPORE HONG KONG TOKYO

ISBN 0 19 211829 3

© *Anne Stevenson 1974*

*Printed in Great Britain by
The Bowering Press Ltd, Plymouth*

To
Caroline, John and Charles

Acknowledgements

Acknowledgements are due to Generation Press, University of Michigan, which published *Living in America* in 1965; and to Wesleyan University Press, which published *Reversals* in 1969. They are also due to the editors of the following journals, in which some of the poems in the third section of this book first appeared: *Counter-Measures, Lines Review, The Listener, The London Magazine, Michigan Quarterly Review, Phoenix, The Scotsman* and *Wave*; and to the editor of the anthology *Dimension I* (1973).

Contents

The Women

Women, waiting for their husbands,
sit among dahlias all the afternoons,
while quiet processional seasons
drift and subside at their doors like dunes,
and echoes of ocean curl from the flowered wall.

The room is a murmuring shell of nothing at all.
As the fire dies under the dahlias, shifting embers
flake from the silence, thundering when they fall,
and wives who are faithful waken bathed in slumber;
the loud tide breaks and turns to bring them breath.

At five o'clock it flows about their death,
and then the dahlias, whirling
suddenly to catherine wheels of surf,
spin on their stems until the shallows sing,
and flower pools gleam like lamps on the lifeless tables.

Flung phosphorescence of dahlias tells
the women time. They wait to be,
prepared for the moment of inevitable
good evening when, back from the deep, from the mystery,
the tritons return and the women whirl in their sea.

To My Daughter in a Red Coat

Late October. It is afternoon.
My daughter and I walk through the leaf-strewn
corridors of the park
in the light and the dark
of the elms' thin arches.

Around us the brown leaves fall and spread;
small winds stir the minor dead;
dust powders the air.
Those shrivelled women stare
at us from their cold benches.

Child, your mittens tug at your sleeves.
(They lick your drumming feet, the leaves.)
You come so fast, so fast;
you violate the past,
my daughter, as your coat dances.

Living in America

"Living in America",
the intelligent people at Harvard say,
"is the price you pay for living in New England."

Californians think
living in America is a reward
for managing not to live anywhere else.

The rest of the country?
Could it be sagging between two poles,
tastelessly decorated, dangerously overweight?

No. Look closely.
Under cover of light and noise
both shores are hurrying towards each other.

San Francisco
is already half way to Omaha.
Boston is nervously losing its way in Detroit.

Desperately the inhabitants
hope to be saved in the middle,
pray to the mountains and deserts to keep them apart.

The Dear Ladies of Cincinnati

"Life is what you make it", my half-Italian
grandmother used to say. And remembering how
her purposely ludicrous voice pulled down the exalted
ceilings of my great aunt's castle in Cincinnati
to gipsy proportions, I know that brave cliché
was a legacy from her father. His western dream
was a palace of chequered aprons. Ambition was colour
and doom as he roared through four fortunes, strewing
sheep, gold, horses and diamonds like sawdust
all over Kentucky. Before he died he squandered
his last square hundred on a silver tureen, a peacock
big as a weathervane on its lid. Then what
could his five chaste daughters do but divide up his
    maxims
And marry as well as they could?

                                    Uselessness
was the use they made of their half raw beauty,
and they all found husbands who, liking their women gay,
preserved them in an air-tight empire made of soap
and mattresses. There, for years, they manufactured
their own climate, generated events to keep
everybody laughing. Outside, the luck of Republicans
fluctuated, stocks were uncertain. Sadness perplexed
    them, but
the aunts kept their chins up trying on hats,
called everybody "sugar", remembered the words of hit
    tunes
they'd been courted to, avoided the contagion of thought
so successfully that the game kept time to the music
even as the vanishing chairs put my grandmother out
and sent my sad over-dieted uncles upstairs
trailing cigar-brown panelling into their bedrooms.

Yet the eyes in the gilded frames of their portraits have
          nothing
unpleasant to say. The red wax roses are dusted
but not arranged. The vellum Catullus crumbles
behind the glass doors of the bookcase, frail as the oakleaf
fifty years dead in its cloudy, undulating pages.
And the ladies, the ladies still sit on the stone verandah,
in the bamboo chairs upholstered with chintz geraniums,
with the white painted wrought iron furniture still in
          bloom,
laughing and rocking and talking their father's language
while the city eats and breathes for them in the distance,
and the river grows ugly in their perpetual service.

Fairy Tale

The ladies sit at the table
where the butler hovers and waits,
tittering over the silver,
dangling their pearls in their plates
while wine in their bubbling glasses
drifts up and evaporates.

The gentlemen loosen their trousers
in the leather arms of their chairs,
make love to their whiskies and sodas
and bawl to the girls upstairs,
"We're waiting to start till you join us."
The gay crowd never appears.

The servants drop dead at their stations,
the weeds grow over their heads;
the ladies are changed into lizards,
the lords into quadrupeds,
while the poets get drunk in the kitchen
and the children dream in their beds.

The Grey Land

I must have been there,
and you—and you,
for we were the very landscape
we walked through.

Our helpless eyes,
our hands and lips and ears
were flickering paths we took
through flickering years.

And we were the rooms,
the houses, voices, faces,
colours and lights, our own
familiar places,

merging and moving
through rank, borderless hours
whose acres ripened and died
as they were ours.

Your way and mine
we chose, or thought we chose;
we passed and the swaying foliage
withered and froze.

Touching, talking,
exchanging our breath for wind . . .
lovers and friends, look back
at the land behind,

at all that remains
of the green delirious way;
the orderly rows of grey
and shades of grey

7

where you and you
and I, as in a cage,
stand motionless, formal—names
stained on a page,

while, without odour,
the lifeless, colourless air
thickens with mist as if something
were dying there

and shadowy actions
vanish before we know
what to regret or forgive
in what they show.

The Takeover

What am I to do? Where am I to go?
The house has been entirely taken over by women.
To every corner they have brought their respectable destruction.
Listen and you can hear them bustling in my lost rooms,
sorting the dust into piles, embracing the furniture,
polishing, pummelling, scurrying, complaining,
pulling up the papers like weeds.
                              Impossible to know
how not to enrage them. Their rules are exuded
inaudibly, vapours which congeal into speech
only when misunderstood. They are like music.
Every woman is an orchestra. Or an explorer,
a discoverer of uninhabitable moods. If they love me
it may be because I divest them of boredom.
I am useful as a conductor of superfluous energies.
But how through their wire-like waists and wrists
do their quick lusts slip, unresisted, into my lap?
Why do I allow them to litter my mind?

They moved in politely, not knowing who I was.
How pretty they were, flitting from mirror to mirror
in their gauze dresses. How delightful and thoughtful.
I should have known when they said they liked me
they liked tidying up messes, that they needed
rooms to have taste in, that little red pulses
beat I, I, I, under the most delicate skin.
Silence is what they're afraid of. They take precautions
always to move in a pack. Knowing also that loneliness
never attacks an argument, all the mothers
and sisters and daughters glare suspiciously
at each other over the tall generations, even when
they seem to be writing letters or playing the piano.

Not one of them forgets for a moment
I am able to escape. They make it my fault

that they have locked themselves up in my house.
They hate my free tempers and private indulgences.
But only the saint or the reprobate need not let
affection affect him. If I were a good man or
a bad man, I think I could make them leave. As it is,
they have made me believe in their attentions. I don't know
what I would want to replace them if they should go.

The Suburb

No time, no time,
and with so many in line to be
born or fed or made love to, there is no
excuse for staring at it, though it's spring again
and the leaves have come out looking
limp and wet like little green new born babies.

The girls have come out in their new bought dresses,
carefully, carefully. They know they're in danger.
Already there are couples crumpled under the chestnuts.
The houses crowd closer, listening to each other's radios.
Weeds have got into the window boxes. The washing hangs,
helpless. Children are lusting for ice cream.

It is my lot each May to be hot and pregnant,
a long way away from the years when I slept by myself—
the white bed by the dressing table, pious with cherry blossoms,
the flatteries and punishments of photographs and mirrors.
We walked home by starlight and he touched my breasts.
"Please, please!" Then I let him anyway. Cars
droned and flashed, sucking at the cow parsley. Later
there were teas and the engagement party. The wedding
in the rain. The hotel where I slept in the bathroom.
The night when he slept on the floor.

The ache of remembering, bitterer than a birth. Better
to lie still and let the babies run through me.
To let them possess me. They will spare me
spring after spring. Their hungers deliver me.
I grow fat as they devour me. I give them my sleep
and they absolve me from waking. Who can accuse me?
I am beyond blame.

Sous-entendu

Don't think

that I don't know
that as you talk to me
the hand of your mind
is inconspicuously
taking off my stocking,
moving in resourceful blindness
up along my thigh.

Don't think
that I don't know
that you know
everything I say
is a garment.

Aubade

Intervention of chairs at midnight.
The wall's approach, the quirkish ambivalence
of photographs, today in daylight,
mere pieces of balance. My brown dress,
tossed, messed, upheld by the floor.
Rags of ordinary washed light
draped as to dry on the brown furniture.
And the big bed reposed, utterly white,
that ached our darkness, rocked our weight.

Love poem

You I embrace,
each eye my face,
hold me now
in my first darkness.
Let me stray through you
to the soft shock
of my beginning.
Stay and be witness
to this fluid rock
cooling and stiffening
in repeated rains.
Also to the sloth of hills building,
to the gathering of mountains.

The Shape of This World

When we loved
it was as if we created each other.
As if in my body two children,
two embryos
curved in the well of my sex.

But then you detached yourself,
you receded, transposed into pure sound—
a bell sharpening itself on its distance,
a blade honing itself to tremulous thinness—
while the mirror held me dumbly—my woman's face,
my body like a globe
nourishing its stray curl of flesh,
my huge breasts and body bound,
bound to the shape of this world.

The Victory

I thought you were my victory
though you cut me like a knife
when I brought you out of my body
into your life.

Tiny antagonist, gory,
blue as a bruise. The stains
of your cloud of glory
bled from my veins.

How can you dare, blind thing,
blank insect eyes?
You barb the air. You sting
with bladed cries.

Snail!   Scary knot of desires!
Hungry snarl!   Small son.
Why do I have to love you?
How have you won?

The Spirit is too Blunt
an Instrument

The spirit is too blunt an instrument
to have made this baby.
Nothing so unskilful as human passions
could have managed the intricate
exacting particulars: the tiny
blind bones with their manipulative tendons,
the knee and the knucklebones, the resilient
fine meshings of ganglia and vertebrae
in the chain of the difficult spine.

Observe the distinct eyelashes and sharp crescent
fingernails, the shell-like complexity
of the ear with its firm involutions
concentric in miniature to the minute
ossicles. Imagine the
infinitesimal capillaries, the flawless connections
of the lungs, the invisible neural filaments
through which the completed body
already answers to the brain.

Then name any passion or sentiment
possessed of the simplest accuracy.
No. No desire or affection could have done
with practice what habit
has done perfectly, indifferently,
through the body's ignorant precision.
It is left to the vagaries of the mind to invent
love and despair and anxiety
and their pain.

After her Death

In the unbelievable days
when death was coming and going
in his only city,
his mind lived apart in the country
where the chairs and dishes were asleep
in familiar positions,
where the geometric faces on the wallpaper
waited without change of expression,
where the book he had meant to come back to
lay open on a bedside table,
oblivious to the deepening snow,
absorbed in its one story.

The Loss

Alive in the slippery moonlight
how easily you managed
to hold yourself upright
on your small heels.
You emerged from your image
on the smooth fields
as if held back from flight
by a hinge.

I used to find you
balanced on your visible ghost,
holding it down by a corner. The blind
stain crawled, fawning, about you.
Your body staked its shadow like a post.
Gone, you leave nothing behind—
not a bone to hold steady or true
your image which lives in my mind.

On Not Being Able to Look
at the Moon

There may be a moon.
Look at the masklike complexion of the roof,
recognizable but relieved of familiarity.
The street, too. How weakened, unstable.
Shadows have more substance than the walls
they lean from. Thick phosphorescence
gathers in the spaces between window
and black window. Something subtle, like a moon,
has been creeping under surfaces,
giving them queer powers of illumination.

In this centreless light
my life might really have happened.
It rises, showing its wounds, longing for
abrasive penances. It touches me with a mania for
stealing moonlight and transforming it into my own pain.
I can feel myself closing like an eye.
I'm unable to look at the moon
or at anything pitted and white that is up there
painted on the sky.

Reversals

Clouds—plainsman's mountains—
islands—inlets—flushed archipelagos—
begin at the horizon's illusory conclusion,
build in the curved dusk
more than what is always imaginary,
less than what is sometimes accessible.
Can you observe them without recognition?

Are there no landscapes at your blurred edges
that change continually away from what they are?
that will not lie, solid, in your clenched eye?
Or is love, in its last metamorphosis, arable,
less than what was sometimes imaginary,
more than what was usually accessible,
full furrows harvested, a completed sky.

England

For Peter Lucas

Without nostalgia who could love England?
Without a sentimental attachment to tolerance
who could delight in this cramped corner country
in no quarter savage, where everything done well
is touched with the melancholy of understanding?

No one leaves England enamoured,
but England remembered invites an equivocal regret.
For what traveller or exile, mesmerized by the sun
or released by spaciousness from habitual self-denial
recalls without wistfulness its fine peculiarities
or remembers with distaste its unique, vulnerable surfaces?

Summer, and the shine of white leaves against thunder.
Ploughland where the wind throws the black soil loose
and horses pull clumsily as though through surf
or stand, hoofs clapped to the earth like bells,
braced in their pastures between churches and seagulls.
England.   Cool and in bloom,
where the light grows like grass out of the ground,
where the sky begets colours on uneasy seasons
and the hills lie down patiently in the rain.

Nowhere as in England is severity cherished
for its own sake or loneliness so compatible.
Where wilderness is scarcer than gardens,
bare land is less dangerous than a cage of chimneys,
and the torn man flies to the small desolations
where the wind can persuade him of vanity
without diminishing his human importance.

Who derives innocence from the rain, from the broken
silences of sheep, from houses lonely in an acre
on the smudged margins of centuries
can never be wholly the prisoner of himself,
hero or victim of his closed, difficult story.

His tragedy, like the sun, is oblique, precarious.
It occurs like a mistake, a reason for embarrassment,
a blunder in the saving ritual of endurance,
and therefore is forgiven and absorbed at last
into the soft sound of the rain.

Americans like England to live in her cameo,
a dignified profile attached to a past
understood to belong to her, like the body of a bust.
The image to the native is battered but complete,
the cracked clay flaking, reluctantly sloughed away,
inadequately renewed on her beautiful bones.

The stinginess of England. The proliferating ugliness.
The pale boys, harmful, dissatisfied, groping for comfort
in the sodium darkness of December evenings.
Wet roofs creeping for miles along wet bricks.
Lovers urgently propping each other on the endless
identical pavements in the vacant light
where the cars live, their pupilless eyes
turned upward without envy or disapproval.

Someone must live in the stunted houses behind the stucco.
Someone must feed from the tiny sick shops.
Someone must love these babies.

                             Unbelievable
in the murk of her cottage, the eighty-year virgin
fussing over bottles and cats. The uncharitable cold.
Light falling in squares from the frugal windows
of public houses. Schoolgirls dragging in crocodile
through the damp lanes behind the converted castle,
querulous in the big wind. In the same wind
that gathers them, together with the pylons and steeples
and gas drums, with the domes and scaffoldings and
      graveyards
and the small kempt gardens by the railway, helplessly,
recklessly, untidily into the temporary spring.

Anglers appear, umbrellas and transistors
in the paths by the silted canals. And Sunday couples,
spread like wet clothes on the banks.
Days unobtrusively seep into the nights,
days that drew the daffodil after the crocus
and lit the rose from the embers of the hyacinth,
thrust nettle and thistle through the ribs of abandoned
        machinery
and green the thick trunks of elaborate beeches.
Then the hills fill with gold wheat.

September.   Already autumnal.
Lost days drift in shapes under the plane trees.
Leaves tangle in the gutters.
In Greenwich, in Kew, in Hampstead
the paths are dry, the ponds dazed with reflections.
Come with me.   Look.   The city
nourished by its poisons, is beautiful in them.
A pearly contamination strokes the river
as the cranes ride or dissolve in it,
and the sun dissolves in the hub of its own explosion.

That there should still be this.
Though memory and anticipation choose
their own images of what has been or could be,
the seconds strike and are gone.
The season is gone that was a long time coming.
The fulfilment is like bread,
and the cornfields lie naked in the burnt shires.

No, not an end. A semblance of ending.
The change is without pause, is perfectly circular,
and the hand that breaks it is the hand that draws.
But we must believe the blunt evidence of our senses
as any physicist the map of his calculations,
as any child the reasonable comfort of his mother
that the leaves are beautiful because they are dying,
that the trees are only falling asleep.

Sierra Nevada

For Margaret Elvin

Landscape without regrets whose weakest junipers
strangle and split granite, whose hard, clean light
is utterly without restraint, whose mountains can purify
and dazzle, and every minute excite us but
never can offer us commiseration, never can tell us
anything about ourselves except that we are dispensable . . .

The rocks and water.
The glimmering rocks and the hundreds
and hundreds of blue lakes ought to be mythical,
while the great trees, as soon as they die,
immediately become ghosts,
stalk upright among the living with awful composure.
But even these bones that the light has taken and twisted,
with their weird gesticulations and shadows that look
as if they had been carved out of dust, even these
have nothing to do with what we have done or not done.

Now, as we climb on the high bare slopes,
the most difficult earth supports the most delicate flowers:
gilia and harebells, kalmia and larkspur, everywhere
the lupin's tight blue spires
and fine-fingered handshaped leaves.
Daintiest of all, the low mariposa, lily of the mountain,
with its honey stained cup and no imperfect dimension.
Strangest and highest, purple and yellow mosses
drink from their own furry stems.

If we stand in the fierce but perfectly transparent wind
we can look down over the boulders, over the drifted scree
with its tattered collar of manzanita,
over the groves of hemlock,
the tip of each tree resembling an arm

extended to a drooping forefinger,
down, down, over the whole, dry, difficult
train of the ascent, down to the lake
with its narrow, swarming edges where the little white boats
are moving their oars like waterbugs.

Nothing but the wind makes noise.
The lake, transparent to its greeny brown floor,
is everywhere else bluer than the sky.
The boats hardly seem to touch its surface. Just as
this granite is something that does not really touch us,
although we stand on it and see the colour of its flowers.
The wind is strong without knowing that it is wind.
The twisted tree that is not warning or supplicating
never considers that it is not wind.
We think that if we were to stay here for a long time,
lie here like wood on these waterless beaches,
we would forget our names, would remember that
what we first wanted had something to do with stones,
the sun, the thousand colours of water,
brilliances,   blues.

New York

This addiction!
The ones who get drunk on it easily!
The romantic, sad-hearted,
expensive inhabitants
who have to believe there is no way out,
who tear at themselves and each other
under the drumbeats while everyone
dances   or weeps
or takes off clothes hopefully,
half sure that the quivering bedstead
can bring forth leaves,
that love, love, love
is the only green in the jungle.

In Italia

Crazy birds in the blues of the campanile
circling in sunlight the rings of orange and amber
terraces dropped like haloes over the houses.
Umbria. Hoods of goldfish scales. But under
the glory, shaggy dwellings with deep claws
clinging to Paradise shaped like a wide wheel.
Christ enthroned at the hub with the glimmering Virgin.
And saints stiff with respect among musical angels.
At the dangerous edges, the praying throng of the saved
crushed into places on the disk circling the stage,
spun out over the waste where the damned writhe
in crazy circles and orange fires burn.

Utah

Somewhere nowhere in Utah, a boy by the roadside,
gun in his hand, and the rare dumb hard tears flowing.
Beside him, the greyheaded man has let one arm slide
awkwardly over his shoulder, is talking and pointing
at whatever it is, dead, in the dust on the ground.

By the old parked Chevy, two women, talking and watching.
Their skirts flag forward. Bandannas twist with their hair.
Around them some sheep and a fence and the sagebrush burning
and burning with its blue flame. In the distance, where
the mountains are clouds, lightning, but no rain.

Dreaming of Immortality in a Thatched Hut

(After the painting by Chin Ch'ang-t'ang)

Drowsing over his verses or drifting
lazily through the sutras,
he blinked in the hazy August silence
through which a blind stream bore on
and the locusts endlessly sawed, performing mistakes
and catching themselves up again like nervous musicians.

The soft rain dropped on the dust at nightfall,
dawns poured revelations over the peaks
until, as he slept, he could see it all—
the graceful ascent from the shelving eaves of the hut.
The ease of detachment. The flowing out of his sleeves.
The slow half sorrowful movement of regret
as he rose with the steadying mists about his knees,
away from the rocks and the stunted, gripping pine
and the books stacked neatly out of the way of the rain.

In March

The snow melts
exposing what was
buried there all winter—
tricycles and
fire-engines and
all sizes of children
waiting in boots and
yellow mackintoshes
for the mud.

The Garden of Intellect

It's too big to begin with.
There are too many windless gardens
walled to protect eccentric vegetation
from a crude climate.
Rare shoots, reared in glass until
old enough to reproduce themselves,
wholly preoccupy the gardeners
who deliberately find it difficult
to watch each other, having planted themselves
head downwards, spectacles
in danger of falling off over their thumbs.

Some beds bear nearly a thousand petunias.
Others labour to produce one rose.
Making sense of the landscape, marking distinctions,
neat paths criss-cross politely,
shaping mauve, indigo and orange hexagons,
composing triangles and circles
to make the terrain seem beautiful.

But to most of the inhabitants
these calculated arrangements are
not only beautiful but necessary.
What they cultivate protects, is protected from
the man-eating weeds of the wilderness,
roses of imaginary deserts,
watered by mirage, embellished
by brilliant illusory foliage, more real
for having neither name nor substance.

The Watchers

It is wise of our enemy to rely upon the watchers.

Wired with a precision that makes nerves anachronisms,
controlled from tall skeletons of electromagnetic steel,
they are dangerous without risk to themselves.
They envisage no distinction.
They anticipate no destruction.
           They are not alive.
Yet they have ears and eyes no
rustle escapes, no flicker misses.

They hover at a level above breathable air,
         but are also near,
in our shoes and telephones.
In our pillows.   In our spoons.
Even when we say nothing,
what passes in our brains
is traced in encephalogram by their ticking.
We are aware of them when we make love.

And because they are unapproachable through anguish,
inaccessible to madness as to argument,
we are more afraid of them than of the great holocaust.
Yet hating and fearing them as we do,
it is curious how often we are exhilarated.
It is as if we had acquired new souls.
Have we forgotten how to be bored?
Are we delivered forever from loneliness?
Are we worthy, we wonder, of the marvel of such attention?

Travelling Behind Glass

Then I spent a long time
living in the mountains
but left them and their silence
unexplored. It was no use
looking to them for mercy.
Caves are not mouths.
Stones are not breasts.
The sun is not an eye.
A scum of blue lichen
may be the only living
possession of the mountains.
Now I am safe behind glass
and driving south.
These are the plains.

How well I know them,
comforters and friends.
Miles that unfold and hold me,
warm and wet and hedged and
swarming with vegetables.
And fat people, farm people
tuning the land with their ploughs
before playing it,
plucking their fields like instruments.

Am I swallowing the road or
am I what the road swallows?
The sweet seeding grass sways
silver as I pass.
Over the ripe wheat
birds gather like snow.
Black snow on the horizon
gathers and flows.

The valleys repeat until
they are like the sea. They

copy its aerial complexion;
islands of ochres and blues
flatten themselves beneath me
into their map. Surf-like scrub
embroiders the clean continents.
Farmhouses, icebergs, lie
as if applied by a hand.

I would ask such a sea
to be accommodating,
to warm me, obey me,
accept me like an arm,
in time to release me
entirely, as nothing at all.
As belonging to nothing at all.

I imagine a life here,
felicitous.
A heart at grass.
A mind at ease in its corner.
Nothing but at morning and evening
the shadows' predictable greens
on the greener ground.
Seed time and harvest time,
in time the night,
and sleep, the good food,
the right nourishment.

And everything could be true:
the walled farmhouses,
the stone bridges,
and towns advancing, daubed,
through the washed sunlight;
blown, scudding fragments of crowd
hauled tight by a market-place,
and cobblestones, lapping or
floating a vast cathedral . . .
possible . . .

Until stopping makes them
property. Somebody's
chickens and beans.
A countable number of sheep.
Telephone wires to the house eaves.
And I have no name in this village
and no one to meet.

*　　*　　*　　*　　*

Who is that woman?

That old woman sitting,
no, moving now,
moving her memories . . .
one black pane,
then another . . . in the
shadow-broken mirror
of her window?

Avoiding her eyes,
I discover my own in her face.
There beside the parked cars
and passing cars,
between the glass and the
prams gorged with babies.

But never whole babies.
Never whole cars.
Parts of them missing.
Parts of them eaten away
where her room—or
is it my eye?—has entered
in a dresser . . . a curtain . . .
a cat with one haunch
through a motorcycle.

I can believe in the cat
and in the motorcycle,
in her and in the
street that intersects her.

But only if the glass were
shattered and the vision
remained could I really
believe in the void between
my time and hers,
in the absence, pieced
out with recollections,
of all her years.

*   *   *   *   *

Sealed in this
carapace, my will
hurtles at seventy,
warm and still
through familiar urban
overspill.
Now and then some
shards, debris, a
tamed, vestigial century;
gabled mansion,
timbered inn,
salvaged church in a
green pen,
steeple raised to
warn or greet
a city crawling
for its meat,
staccato, crawling
red and neat,
home to its plural
human street.

This must be a place to
pass through, on the way
somewhere, or away.
Nowhere to make a home in,
though women may have hung
pure passion on the lines,

and men have it in their minds,
come evening, to come back here,
breaking the opaque,
continuously equal membrane
into a solace or anguish
of their own.

There is just enough room.
Behind each pair of curtains,
enough and no more,
for the wanting and having,
for the having and sacrifice,
for each day keeping its balance
on the shelf between meal and meal,
waking and cooking and eating
to an endless beginning
in the square bed,
trim as a cake or an altar
under its lavender,
cruel as an altar
under its wreath of roses.

And which is the street?
And which the number?
Behind which window
does the woman myself
multiply out of her noon
into three children,
divide and reconstitute
in the flesh of three children
where is just enough room
for this day and the next day,
where the paranoid howl of the
highway troubles the
far side of the glass
without breaking it,
whines behind the frost
of the window, not
touching her at all,

not disturbing for an instant
the monotony of her purpose
or the respectability
of her sacrifice.

How easy to accept,
to be content
with her invitation . . .
They were so beautiful,
your children, in the park,
rolling down that embankment
into a blackness of rhododendrons.

But how will you describe the
conspicuous hush of the suburbs
when the children have grown
up and gone?
Your breasts sag into your ribs.
You dig weeds out of the lawn.
The radio's on . . .

*   *   *   *   *

A wider view is this estuary, an entrance.
In the distance, three
erect, steaming chimneys,
part of the steel works.
Pylons, six shoulders to each,
six skeletal shivas.
They have taken with indifference
the prim, sacred cities of the old maps,
forcing the small passages.
Mariages de convenance.

A used country
wanting to be used.
Its history, a shell
broken, like this castle,
on the jaw of a hill
down which the cracked

chalk houses spill, an
avalanche arrested.
Hope lies at the bottom
in the valley of roofs.

Follow them, children,
cultivate the roofs as they
circle through their new and
grey necessary pastures.
Between highway and highway and
highway there may be a door.

But I have forgotten what
home it was I came for.
My body's a cave and my
two breasts are stones,
and this sun is so dull and
estranged that I know
this dark glass as
the only living possession of the valley.

It dreams that the
pith and the core of this
too precious island
shudder into space
with the candour of any volcano,
while I drive alone and alive
on the oily circumference,
peering at the twittering abyss,
l'abîme des oiseaux,
until the glass shatters (loud iridescence)
into its stars, and the stars
scatter, flashing like kingfishers,
into the emptiness.

The Crush

Handsome as D'Artagnan,
inaccessible as Mr. Darcy,
she observes him in the bulge of her
mother's teapot . . . once.
There are other views. Church.
He, robed in the choir. She
behind hats, among pews.
Her eyes grope towards him,
swerve, avoid the
impossible terror of his attention.
Weekdays she wanders near his house.
He pounds the piano.
The *Fantasiestücke* weigh within her
like a dangerous possession.

41

The Marriage

They will fit, she thinks,
but only if her backbone
cuts exactly into his rib cage,
and only if his knees
dock exactly under her knees
and all four
agree on a common angle.

All would be well
if only
they could face each other.

Even as it is
there are compensations
for having to meet
nose to neck
chest to scapula
groin to rump
when they sleep.

They look, at least,
as if they were going
in the same direction.

The Affair

He moves off at dawn,
away from the swollen sheets,
the room like a stage, its hooded light
extravagant with gestures and features,
its revelations already hurrying away from them
as they stand and dress.

Only a door's breadth between himself
and the widening greyness. The houses
flatten themselves a little into their limbo.
A blackbird, tentatively. The first car.
A light on, yellow, in an upstairs window.

These things as they are,
on the scaffolding just as they are,
of the night beneath them.

The Demolition

They have lived in each other so long
there is little to do there.
They have taken to patching the floor
while the roof tears.

The rot in her feeds on his woodwork.
He batters her cellar.
He camps in the ruins of her carpet.
She cries on his stairs.

Old Scholars

They have written it
all in their minds a thousand times,
so neither believes that
the wound behind his lips can be
healed by her lips, or that
he could come out of the storm,
from the leaves in October,
to find in her lap
what her eyes give him
easily and lazily. All the same,
here they are—two thumbed manuscripts—
remembering mainly the
work of it, mainly
the work of it.

On the Edge of the Island

Wherever there is land ending and an ocean begins . . .
whenever these meet, not alive, like some satisfied jig-saw,
one map, without wind, without rock,
without memories of weathers or of sons and fathers,
or of beaches in their death-frills, or of fearers and watchers,
there are always one or two taken in,
there are always just a few who go back,

just a few who hanker still
for the peephole through the mortar of the will
that shows you you needn't be at all.
There, at the end of the uncertain road,
where the sea stands up like a level hill,
the lighthouse dispenses its marginal salvation.
White birds, without names, call and call.

Coming Back to Cambridge

Casual, almost unnoticeable,
it happens every time you return.
Somewhere along the flat road in
you lose to the voluptuous levels,
between signposts to unnecessary dozing villages
every ghost of yourself but Cambridge.
Somewhere—by Fen Drayton or Dry Drayton,
by the finger pointed aimlessly to Over—
you slip into a skin that lives
perpetually in Cambridge.

It knows where you are.

As you drive you watch a workman
wheel his bicycle around a stile,
hump onto the saddle and
ride off past a field of cows.
A few stop chewing to stare.
And you know where you are even before
landmarks (beautiful to the excluded)
begin to accumulate.
The stump of the library.
The lupin spire of the Catholic Church.
Four spikey blossoms on King's.
The Round Church, a mushroom in this
forest of Gothic and traffic and
roses too perfect to look alive.

The river is the same—conceited,
historic, full of the young.
The streets are the same. And around them
the same figures, the same cast with a
change of actors, move as if concentric
to a radiance without location.
The pupils of their eyes glide sideways,

apprehensive of martyrdom to which
they might not be central.
They can never be sure.
Great elations could be happening without them.

And just as the hurrying, preoccupied dons
tread the elevations of their detachment and yet
preserve an air of needing to be protected,
so, also, these wives choosing vegetables in the market,
these schoolchildren in squadrons,
these continental girl-friends and black men,
these beards, these bicycles, these
skinny boys fishing, these lovers of the pubs,
these lovers of the choirboys, these intense shrill
ladies and gaunt, fanatical burnt out old women
are all more than this . . . arrogant . . .
within the compass of wistfulness.

Nothing that really matters really exists.

But the statues are alive.
You can walk in and out of the picture.
Though the mild facades harden before and
behind you like stereographs, within them
there is much to be taken for granted.
Meals and quarrels. Passions and inequalities.
A city like any other . . . were it not for the
order at the centre and the
high, invisible bridge it is built upon
with its immense views of an intelligible human landscape
into which you never look without longing to enter;
into which you never fall without the curious struggle back.

Siskin

Small bird with green plumage,
yellow to green to white
on the underparts, yes, a siskin
alive on my own cedar,
winter visitor, resident in Scotland,
wholly himself.

I saw him, and you, too,
alive again,
thin but expert, seated
with your bird-glasses, bird book
and concentrated expression,
hoping for siskins in Vermont.

He pleased me for your sake—
not so much as he would have pleased you.
Unless it was you he came for
and I something you inhabited
from the second his green flame
flickered in that black tree
to the next second
when he was gone.

Generations

Know this mother by her three smiles.
One grey one drawn over her mouth by frail hooks.
One hurt smile under each eye.

Know this mother by the frames she makes.
By the silence in which she suffers each child
to scratch out the aquatints in her mind.

Know this mother by the way she says
"darling" with her teeth clenched.
By the fabulous lies she cooks.

At Thirteen

Woodsmoke

and in those soft legal hollows
nothing but
the sanest odours.
Even at sundown
nothing but the
gentlest scents.

Then the young girl
flows in out of the twilight,
hair streaming, part of her streaming,
new breasts held like breath and yet swelling,
arms witheld, aching, yet waiting,
so, like a river,
into the deep light room.

Where now light possesses her.
Diaphanous accusation.
Eyes harden to reflectors.
Angers stagnate in her throat.
No speech but a cry.
Then a slammed door . . .

Leaving

the mother who has done so little . . .
fetched a daysoaked shirt out of the basin,
offered her chicken and rice,
smiled at her vaguely, or kindly
over some wall of book . . . who

pinioned to that small stony shadow
can be nothing but
reproach to her.

51

Withering slimness.
Used breasts, closed volumes of slimness.
Nothing but reproach to her.
Declaration of fear.

Theme with Variations

Distractions, considerations.
There are so many.
There is money.
There are possessions.
There are the professions and inventions.
And there are the men alone,
and forever those
soft thighs thought of and thought of
in empty rooms.
For there only is one love
which is never enough.

Evasions, sophistications.
They have a use.
There is booze.
There is titivation.
There is the fox on the flesh
where the breast pushes up to the throat.
There is the flash
in the groin and the long meal's
anecdote . . .
but only the one love
which is ever real.

Ovations. O deprivations!
Such semen has crept
into blonde violins,
rich horns, shy string quartets
out of Beethoven's furious genitals,
and Schubert's
and Mozart's,
that ladies who bend to their cellos,
their velvet knees apart
know well there can only be one love
which is never Art.

53